Tweed Heads

Brunswick Heads

Clarence River

Yamba

Bellinger Valley

Nambucca Heads

Macleay River

Port Macquarie

Taree

Forster and Tuncurry

Tea Gardens and Hawks Nest

NEW SOUTH WALES

Newcastle

Gosford
Woy Woy

Brisbane Water
Broken Bay

SYDNEY

Port Jackson
Botany Bay

Wollongong

Shoalhaven River

Kiama

Nowra

Huskisson and Jervis Bay

Ulladulla

Bateman's Bay

Narooma

Bermagui

Eden

Twofold Bay

Boydtown

Norfolk Island

SYDNEY

To. Len
Thanks For.
Comming.
All Our Love.
Jim Pam & Family
1983.

COASTAL TOWNS

of New South Wales
and Norfolk Island

Cedric Emanuel

Cassell Australia

CAPTAIN JAMES COOK, R.N.

Captain James Cook R.N.

In 1770 the honour of making known to the world the whole eastern seaboard of Australia fell to James Cook. The one-time farm boy and grocer's assistant was born on 27 October 1728 in Yorkshire, England. Cook was speared to death by natives on an Hawaiian beach in 1779, nine years after stepping ashore at Botany Bay. He was undoubtedly one of the greatest navigators of all time.

H.M.S. *Endeavour*'s journal shows entry by Captain James Cook of landing at Botany Bay, April 1770.

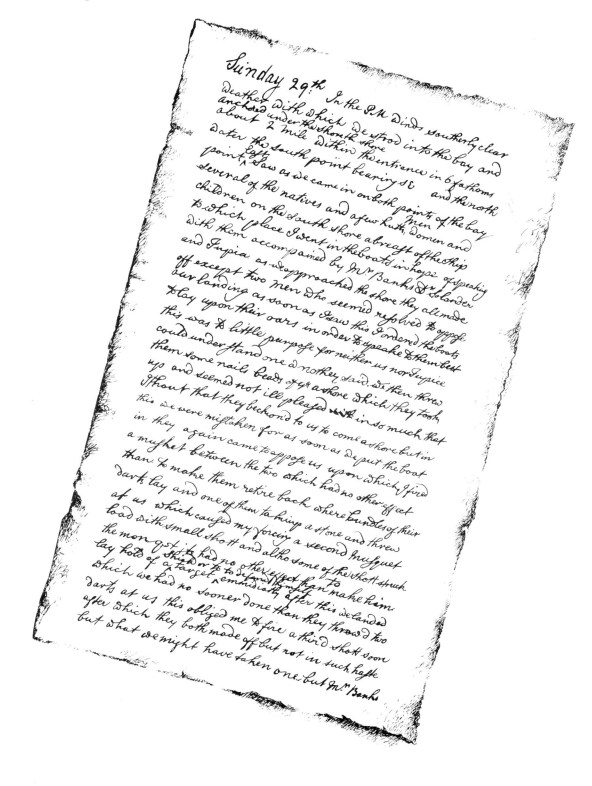

Cassell Australia Limited
44 Waterloo Road North Ryde NSW 2113
30 Curzon Street North Melbourne Victoria 3051
in association with Cassell Limited, Auckland

Copyright © 1980 Cedric Emanuel

First published 1980
Designed by Kim Falkenmire
Set by B&D Modgraphic in 12/13 Sabon
Printed and bound by Times Printers, Singapore

National Library of Australia
Cataloguing-in-Publication Data

Emanuel, Cedric, 1906–
    Coastal towns of New South Wales and Norfolk
    Island.
    Index
    ISBN 0 7269 2669 8

    1. New South Wales—Description and travel.
    2. Cities and towns—New South Wales.
    3. Norfolk Island—Description and travel.
    I. Title.

919.44′0463

CONTENTS

INTRODUCTION

The title of this book suggests that I have dealt with only coastal towns but I have, with an artist's licence, included in brief, one or two of the numerous beautiful valleys that are situated on the coastal strip between the Pacific Ocean and the Great Dividing Range. This mountain range extends the length of the coast and occasionally juts into the sea, as it does on the Illawarra section of the coast. Both south and north I found delightful valleys such as the Jamberoo near Kiama, and the Bellinger near Nambucca Heads, and I understood well why these places had attracted the attention of artists, both from Australia and overseas.

The shift away from river and sea transport has emphasized the importance of the railway and the Princes and Pacific Highways. James Cook charted the coast from the sea and was followed by many others, and for decades after settlement the only access to the coastal settlements was by boat. Later, river transport—droghers, sail and steam vessels—ferried people and supplies up and down the rivers and punts and rowboats took them across rivers. Now the coastal ships have mostly gone, the punts have been replaced by bridges and the towns are linked by road and in many instances by rail. In making this book I travelled on Route I—Eden to Sydney (496 kilometres) on the Princes Highway, and then Sydney to Tweed Heads (894 kilometres) on the Pacific Highway. I was rewarded with stunning coastal scenery, bold mountain escarpments, lush valleys, sand dunes, surging seas, peaceful lakes, sea lagoons and glistening beaches. The last owe their popularity in no small measure to the members of the 117 Surf Life Saving Clubs in N.S.W. who give voluntary service from October to April each year.

Although governments at all levels receive much criticism for not preserving more of our natural environment, one is surprised to find when travelling the length of the coast that provision has been made for extensive public parks, state forests, reserves and campsites where travellers or holidaymakers can escape and enjoy the beauty of headland, beach, river and sea. The more the public concerns itself with its environment, the more authorities will consider public needs, and maybe one day permanent caravan parks will not marr some of our finest headlands and beaches and waterways will not be polluted. It is up to us to preserve one of the most beautiful coastlines in the world for ourselves and future generations.

Cedric Emanuel

EDEN, BOYDTOWN AND TWOFOLD BAY

Eden, 496 kilometres south of Sydney on the Princes Highway, is the last big town before the Victorian border. Eden sits on a peninsula headland between the graceful sweeping arms of Twofold Bay. At Boyd Town, on the southern arm of the bay, 11 kilometres away from Eden, are the remains of the big bold dreams of the British entrepreneur, Benjamin Boyd.

Twofold Bay was discovered by George Bass in 1797 and the following year Bass and Matthew Flinders surveyed the area. The earliest whaling operation in the bay was that of Raine and Irvine in 1828 and they were followed in the early 1840s by Benjamin Boyd and a little later, the Imlay brothers.

Eden was selected as the official townsite in 1842, but for some time it was overshadowed by Ben Boyd's sister towns of Boyd Town and East Boyd. This changed, however, when Boyd left the district in 1850 after the spectacular collapse of his financial empire.

The discovery of gold at Kiandra in 1860 brought a short-lived boom to the town and bay, but after this the area settled back to timber-getting, fishing and some dairying.

There are five commercial ports on the New South Wales coast. Eden is a major oil depot where tankers discharge fuel and cargo ships load wood chips that are milled near Boydtown and are destined for Japan.

Woodchips Industry
Twofold Bay

EDEN
Twofold Bay

Cedric Emanuel

BERMAGUI

1166 lb
Black
Marlin

Bermagui is a small, meandering village surrounded by
the sea, the Bermagui River and forested mountains. It is
389 kilometres south of Sydney and is a very popular
holiday resort for campers, fishermen and surfers. An
early plan of the settlement has it marked as Permageua
but somehow it became Bermagui, an Aboriginal word
which means, depending on your reference, 'canoe with
paddles' or 'canoe without paddles'.

The village was planned in 1867 and has a population
of about 900. Local industries include timber, tourism
and fishing—especially for tuna and abalone. Gold was
found in the area in the 1860s at Mount Dromedary,
and just outside north Bermagui the vertical shafts left
behind by the Chinese miners can still be seen. The
town's water supply comes from a natural spring on the
impressive Mount Dromedary, which was named by
James Cook in 1770.

Zane Grey gave the village some international fame in
the 1930s in his book *An American Angler in Australia*,
and several landmarks in Bermagui perpetuate his
memory.

Bermagui N.S.W.

Bermagui
Fishermen

Bermagui south coast N.S.W.
Cedric Emanuel

5

NAROOMA

The attractive and busy town of Narooma is 350 kilometres south of Sydney on the Princes Highway. Surveyed in 1883, it was named after Thomas Forster's cattle station *Noorooma*, which is an Aboriginal word meaning 'blue water'. The town, which is in two sections, became known as Narooma and was officially renamed in 1972. Narooma's smaller section is on the Wagonga River flats, south of the Wagonga River bridge. The larger commercial section is on the hill overlooking the river.

Narooma has a population of about 2000; this is swelled annually by the large number of visitors who come to enjoy the fishing and swimming delights of the river and seashore and the other tourist facilities available. Besides tourism and big-game fishing, local industries include oyster-farming, abalone-diving, fishing and timber-getting.

Fosters Bay - Narooma

Narooma - South Coast N.S.W

Looking Glass rock.

NAROOMA

BATEMAN'S BAY

Bateman's Bay is a large inlet which tapers after about 6 kilometres to become the entrance to the Clyde River. The town of Bateman's Bay is charmingly situated on the south side of the river near the bridge, a vertical lift span which opens for river traffic.

In 1770 James Cook noted the bay as he journeyed north along the coast and named it after Nathaniel Bateman, who had been captain of the ship *Northumberland*. Cedar-cutters were the next Europeans to come to the area, and in 1821 Alexander Berry examined the bay and river but he subsequently settled further north near Nowra. The region was settled in the 1830s, but development was slowed after 1837 because the nearby settlement of Broulee was surveyed and it became the centre of shipping activity in the area. The decline of the coastal trade meant progress for Bateman's Bay because its road link made it more convenient.

The main products of the Bateman's Bay district are cheese and milk, vegetables, fish, oysters and timber. Tourism is a growing industry with visitors coming mainly from Sydney, 282 kilometres to the north, and from the Canberra district inland.

Cedric Emanuel

Bateman's Bay. N.S.W.

Batemans Bay

An early Timber Mill at Batemans Bay.

9

ULLADULLA

The busy fishing port and tourist resort of Ulladulla is 230 kilometres south of Sydney on the Princes Highway. Delightfully located at the end of a long string of coastal lakes and lagoons with mountains to the west, the town and its environs are a focal point of tourist activity.

Ulladulla is an Aboriginal word meaning 'safe harbour'. Originally a timber port used for shipping cedar to Sydney in the 1820s, it was surveyed for a townsite in 1837. One of the early settlers was the Reverend Thomas Kendall, grandfather of the poet Henry Kendall, who was born at Kermington near Ulladulla in 1839.

The commercial fishing fleet, made up of fishing trawlers and tuna boats, operates from the picturesque harbour. It has two large walls to stop sand bars from developing and provide protection from rough seas. Ulladulla has a large Italian community mainly involved in commercial fishing. One of the traditions of this group, the blessing of the fishing fleet, has become a colourful event at the beginning of the fishing season.

Ulladulla has a population of more than 4000 and industries other than fishing are timber and dairying.

Old Timber Mill – ULLADULLA – South Coast N.S.W.

The Breakwater Ulla Dulla. South Coast N.S.W.

11

HUSKISSON AND JERVIS BAY

The small fishing port and holiday centre of Huskisson is snugly tucked away on the south bank of the Currambene Creek, near its entrance to the western shore of Jervis Bay. It is 187 kilometres south of Sydney. Jervis Bay was sighted by Cook in 1770, named by Lieutenant John Bowen in 1791 and explored by Lieutenant James Grant in 1801. Governor Macquarie described it as 'a noble capacious bay' when he visited the area in 1811. In 1813 Captain Collins landed at Jervis Bay and tried to reach the Shoalhaven River, but he was thwarted by the extensive swamps. Hamilton Hume in 1821 assessed the area as fertile and judged that he could cut a road through from Sydney to Jervis Bay.

The village of Huskisson was established in 1841 by Governor Gipps and it is thought to have been named after a Colonial Secretary, William Huskisson. Fishing is the main activity and the area is well known for its catches of live bait—especially for fishermen of tuna and pilchards. The unspoilt beauty of Jervis Bay is due in part to the Naval Base established there and to the ardour of conservationists, who opposed a proposed steel mill and nuclear plant in the area. Now, in the 1980s, visitors can still delight in the clear water, the white sandy beaches and natural woodland of Jervis Bay.

The old wharf Huskisson

HUSKISSON RSL CLUB

The Estuary and the Sea
HUSKISSON

NOWRA

Nowra is a bustling tourist centre on the central south coast and the administrative base for the Shoalhaven Shire. Part of the Illawarra coast of New South Wales, Nowra is 163 kilometres south of Sydney, and has a population of approximately 15 500. Situated about 13 kilometres upstream on the south bank of the Shoalhaven River, it is linked to the north bank by an impressive eight-span steel bridge.

Alexander Berry, Nowra's first settler, chose to settle on the north bank when he established his property at the foot of Mount Coolangatta in 1822. Although Berry was originally granted land between the Shoalhaven and Crookhaven Rivers, he applied for, and received, a further grant on the north side. Here he set up his headquarters which he called Coolangatta. Berry supplied cedar and general farm produce to Sydney, but due to various problems and the death of his partner, Edward Wollstonecraft, Berry's interest in the area lessened. In the 1850s he began leasing farms and Nowra began to develop as tenant farmers moved in and local merchants became established. By 1852 a village plan had been approved and five years later the first land was being sold. Nowra was proclaimed a municipal district in 1871. In 1893 the south coast railway from Sydney reached the north side of the river and never went any further, so the small settlement of Berry, named after Alexander Berry, became the rail terminus on the south coast.

The district produces dairy products, vegetables, and timber. Manufacturing plants supply agricultural machinery, rubber goods, paper and flour.

As a tourist centre Nowra is the starting point for many nearby beach and lake resorts; valleys which offer splendid hiking and camping areas, and mountains which give breathtaking views of the coast and the valleys. A special treat for history lovers is the Coolangatta Historical Village: a group of buildings which have been restored and transformed into motel-type units. These were originally part of Alexander Berry's Coolangatta property.

Meroogal, Nowra

The mouth of the Shoalhaven River

Convict Cottage

Old Stables

Notes at the Historic village Coolangatta (near NOWRA)

Conrad Martens drew this village in 1860

KIAMA

Kiama is a delightful small town about 120 kilometres from Sydney on the Illawarra coast. Renowned as a tourist resort, it has many attractions including the spectacular blow-hole, discovered by George Bass in 1797, and behind it, the beautiful Jamberoo Valley with its gentle, grassed farmlands and splendid scenery. In Kiama and the Jamberoo Valley there are many superb blue stone dry walls separating paddocks in a style reminiscent of the English countryside. These were built from 1857 onward by Thomas Newing, a craftsman from Kent in England.

The town has many buildings of historical significance including Hartwell House built by Thomas Chapman in 1858; Mount Vernon built by Henry Connell around 1875; the stately post office (1880) and Christ Church with its unusual cedar ceiling which resembles an upturned boat (1858).

Kiama was discovered by George Bass in 1797 and timber-cutters moved in to take the cedar out as early as 1815. The town was gazetted in 1838 and the rail link with Sydney was opened in 1887. The inadequate open harbour at Kiama was a serious problem for the early settlers, so in 1871 a coffer dam was built to restrain the sea while the Robertson Basin was excavated from the hard basalt rock. The work took five years, but it finally gave some protection for shipping, as did the lighthouse on the headland which began operating in 1887. Now the railway and the road carries the freight to and from Kiama, but the pretty breakwater port is a haven for Kiama's fishing fleet.

Kiama

Post Office Tower

Lighthouse
1887

Kiama.

Farm in Jamberoo Valley

Homestead in the Jamberoo Valley —

Part of the Beautiful Valley
at Jamberoo —

19

WOLLONGONG

Wollongong is one of Australia's largest industrial cities. It is beautifully situated on a narrow coastal strip between the sea and the rugged escarpment of the Illawara Coastal Ridge. The city, with an area of 715 square kilometres, is made up of many smaller centres between Windang in the south, Dapto in the south-west and Helensburg in the north. It is a cosmopolitan city, with a large immigrant population. Along its 64 kilometre sea front, from Lake Illawarra in the south to Stanwell Park in the north, a scalloped chain of glistening sandy beaches is linked by jutting headlands and broad flat rockshelves. The coastal scenery from Lawrence Hargrave Drive is breathtakingly beautiful.

James Cook tried to make a landing on the Illawarra coast in 1770 but he was foiled by the rough surf, whereas George Bass and Matthew Flinders were blown there and landed by accident in 1796. The first Europeans to cross the coastal plain and find coal in the area were the survivors of the *Sydney Cove* wreck in 1797. James Meehan, a government surveyor, reported cedar stands there in 1805 and by 1812 the cedar-cutters were hauling their sawn logs up the scarp face near Bulli. A drought on the Cumberland Plain around Sydney in 1815 led Dr Charles Throsby to the Illawarra Plain in search of grazing land and he settled his stockman in a hut near the present Harbour and Smith Streets. The following year John Oxley surveyed the Five Islands District, as it was then known, and made the first grants of land.

The town was gazetted in 1834, but its major problem was transporting produce to Sydney. A mediocre harbour and the difficulty of hauling goods and timber up the escarpment led to the excavation of Belmore Basin beside the small harbour. Some 300 convicts began work on the basin in 1837 and the excavation and a semi-circular stone wharf and breakwater were finished in 1844. The attractive Belmore Basin Lighthouse was erected in 1871 and it is now classified by the National Trust. A new lighthouse above the harbour on Flagstaff Point was built in 1937.

Wollongong's buildings of historical interest include the Anglican Pro-Cathedral of St Michael (1859) which was designed by the colonial architect, Edmund Blacket; the small stone primary school and teacher's residence at Mount Kiera; the Italianate court house (1880) designed by James Barnet and the brick and stone public school with its distinctive bell tower in Smith Street.

St Michaels Cathedral
(1858 - E.T. BLACKET)
Classified by the National Trust

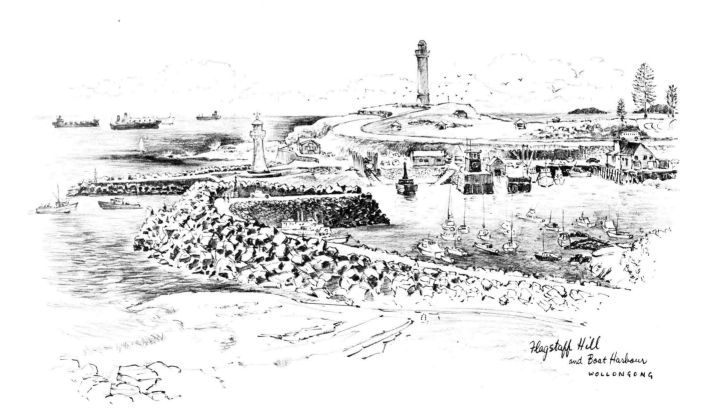

Flagstaff Hill
and Boat Harbour
WOLLONGONG

Belmore Basin Lighthouse 1871
Classified by the National Trust

South Coast Notes

Coalcliff
Port Kembla in distance

CLIFTON

Bulli Veteran
202 Princes Highway

23

BEAUTIFUL BEACHES

GARIE

South Coast. N.S.W

Cedric Emanuel

South Coast Beauty

Bondi
The Baths where many champions learned their swimming.

From Tamarama to Maroubra

Headland AVALON

FROM Bilgola — BEAUTIFUL VIEWS NORTH AND SOUTH

Broken Bay Entrance
from Whale Beach
CENTRAL COAST

A.J. SMALL LOOKOUT
NATIONAL TRUST

BOTANY BAY

Botany Bay, 8 kilometres south of Sydney, is a large shallow bay protected by two peninsulas—La Perouse and Kurnell. Both are government reserves. Originally known as Stingray Bay, it was the first landing place on the Australian continent by James Cook in 1770. Isaac Smith, a midshipman who later became a rear-admiral, is commemorated by a tablet at Kurnell as it is thought he was the first white person ashore from Cook's landing party. The favourable reports of the bay by Cook and his botanist, Sir Joseph Banks, probably influenced the decision to direct Captain Arthur Phillip and the first fleet to establish a penal colony there in 1788. Phillip, however, rejected the bay, mainly because of lack of fresh water, and sailed north to establish his settlement at Port Jackson. He left behind Captain John Hunter who, on 26 January 1788, assisted the French explorer Comte de La Perouse into the bay so that he could repair one of his longboats. Perouse stayed six weeks and his visit is commemorated in the name of the peninsula and by a monument erected there in 1825 by another French explorer, Baron de Bougainville. To deter smugglers and to direct stray vessels, Governor Macquarie had a sandstone watchtower built at La Perouse in about 1820. Across the bay on the Kurnell peninsula there are monuments to the botanists Joseph Banks and D. C. Solander and the grave of the seaman, Forby Sutherland. An obelisk commemorating the centenary of James Cook's landing was erected in 1870.

Today Botany Bay is a busy port. It has been deepened and wharfs have been built to cater for the shipping needs of the oil refinery on the south-east shore. There is also a runway from Kingsford Smith Airport extending into the bay.

Popular pastimes on the bay are sailing and fishing and there are enclosed baths for swimming on the bayside beaches. Attached to La Perouse by a footbridge is Bare Island which Cook described in his journal as 'a small bare island which lies close to the north shore' of Botany Bay. The island was made into a defence battery as a result of the 1877 war between Russia and Turkey. Britain was allied with Turkey at the time and it was thought that the Russian Pacific Fleet might attack British possessions in the area. The defences were built in 1881 and were used for only ten years. They now stand as one of the few examples of fortress architecture in Australia and the island has been declared an historic site.

Classified by the National Trust

Captain Cook's Memorial of landing at Botany Bay

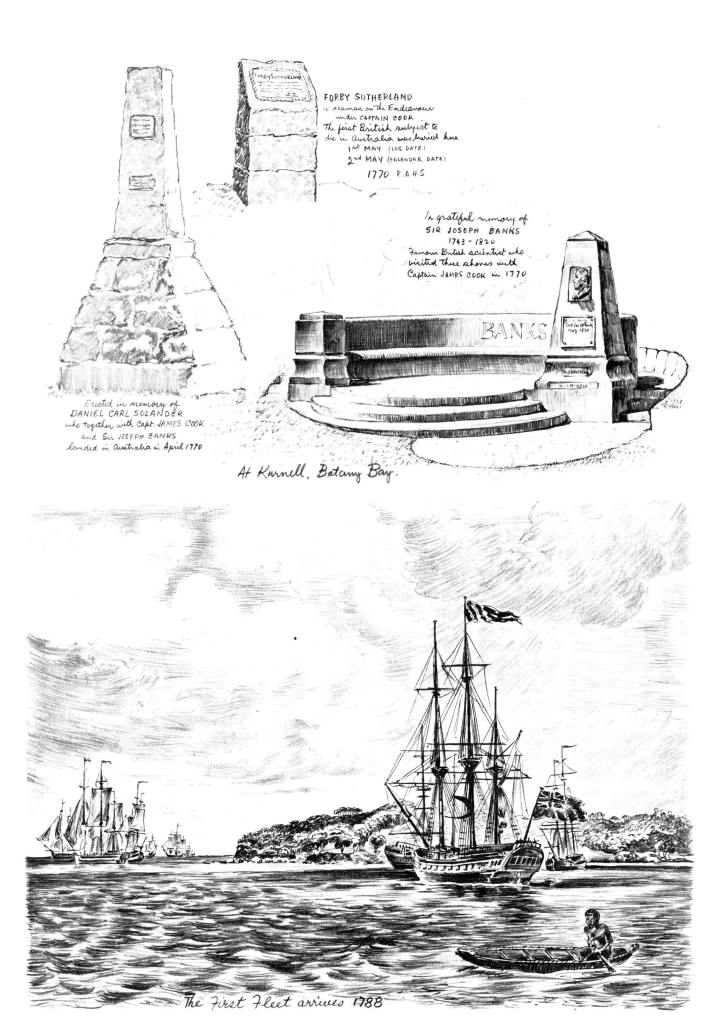

FORBY SUTHERLAND
a seaman on the Endeavour
under CAPTAIN COOK
The first British subject to
die in Australia was buried here
1st MAY (LOG DATE)
2nd MAY (CALENDAR DATE)
1770 R.A.H.S

In grateful memory of
SIR JOSEPH BANKS
1743 - 1820
Famous British scientist who
visited these shores with
Captain JAMES COOK in 1770

BANKS

Erected in memory of
DANIEL CARL SOLANDER
who together with Capt. JAMES COOK
and Sir JOSEPH BANKS
landed in Australia in April 1770

At Kurnell, Botany Bay.

The First Fleet arrives 1788

Bare Island Fort
BOTANY BAY

The Barrack Tower
and Bare Island Fort
BOTANY BAY

Joseph Banks Hotel

Captain Cook Bridge

Pilot and Rescue Boats
BOTANY BAY

SYDNEY, PORT JACKSON

Sydney Harbour is very beautiful and has had a great many superlatives heaped upon it since Captain Arthur Phillip described it, in January 1788, as 'the finest harbour in the world'. The harbour is entered from the sea by passing through two massive sandstone headlands, South Head and North Head. The city and the main shipping wharfage are located on the south side of the harbour. To the west is Middle Harbour and to the north is Manly. The Parramatta River, which is heavily industrialized, and the Lane Cove River drain into the harbour. It is a very busy harbour which is used extensively for commercial shipping, commuter transport and recreation. Within the harbour there are several small islands and one, Garden Island, now joined to the land, is used exclusively by the Navy. Another tiny island, Fort Denison, which was a pyramid-shaped rocky outcrop has had a series of names: Mate-wa-ye by the Aborigines; Rock Island by Arthur Phillip; Pinchgut by many since it was used as a bread-and-water prison in 1789 for convicts who had stolen supplies when all at the settlement were on

The 'Gap' WATSON'S BAY
Scene of the wreck of the 'DUNBAR' 1857.

rations; and finally Fort Denison in honour of Sir W. T. Denison who prepared the plans for the defence of Port Jackson. Fortification work began in 1840 but it was temporarily abandoned and the solid Martello tower, designed to house heavy guns at its top, was finally finished in 1857. Although it has never been used for military purposes, it has been used for storage of navigation signals and for the recording of tides.

On South Head stands the Macquarie Lighthouse, which was originally built by Governor Macquarie to a Francis Greenway design in 1816. This lighthouse was replaced by a replica of the original in 1880. North of this light on Inner South Head stands the Hornby Light which was erected in 1858 and first lit on 31 January 1859. Near the light is an attractive group of small colonial stone cottages. The light was built after the *Dunbar* and *Catherine Adamson* had been wrecked on South Head. At the top of The Gap on South Head there is a memorial in the form of the anchor from the ill-fated *Dunbar* whose hull was torn open by the rocks at the base of the steep cliffs of the gap.

Port Jackson - SYDNEY
Passed by Captain Cook 6ᵗʰ May, 1770

The HORNBY LIGHT and Two Stone Cottages
SOUTH HEAD - Classified by the National Trust

Bradley's Head
SYDNEY HARBOUR
Cedric Emanuel 1979

Fort Denison

Camp Cove where Phillip first landed   Cedric Emanuel

Sydney from Athol Bay

Eric Emanuel
1979

WB
1788

IR
FM

Probably the oldest marks
of white settlement in Australia

F.M. believed to be Frederick Meredith of the H.M.S. SIRIUS. WB & I.R. not known

BROKEN BAY

Broken Bay, 16 nautical miles north of Sydney Harbour, is the estuary of the beautiful Hawkesbury River, the longest coastal river on the east coast of Australia. The Hawkesbury rises at Crookwell, where it is known as the Wollondilly; it then becomes the Warragamba, then the Nepean and after it has been joined by the Grose River it becomes the Hawkesbury. It is a deep winding waterway with wooded banks, steep sided sandstone cliffs and tranquil bays. It has three branches—Pittwater which honours William Pitt the Younger, Cowan Creek and Brisbane Water. At the entrance to Broken Bay is Lion Island, so called because it resembles a crouching lion, and deep inside Pittwater is Scotland Island. There are quite a few smaller islands scattered throughout the estuary. This waterway is one of the most attractive cruising, boating and fishing areas in Australia. The scenery is superb, the water is deep and the area so extensive that solitude is easily found.

Pittwater was described by Captain Arthur Phillip in 1788 as 'the finest piece of water I ever saw'. Across from Barranjoey Headland at the tip of the Pittwater Peninsula is West Head which is also known as Commodore Heights. From here magnificent panoramas of the splendours of Broken Bay can be seen. On Barranjoey Headland, reached by a walk along a sandspit which tied an island to the peninsula, is situated the impressive sandstone Barranjoey Lighthouse built in 1881 designed by the colonial architect, James Barnet. This lighthouse, one of the two stone lighthouses on the New South Wales coast, replaced two wooden towers built in 1879. Arthur Phillip sheltered in a cave near the present Pittwater jetty during his explorations of the area in 1789. The area was settled in the 1840s and a customs house set up in 1843 at Barranjoey was used until the turn of the century.

The grandeur of the scenery and the facilities for recreation bring thousands of people each year to Broken Bay for sailing, swimming, fishing or just messing about in boats.

Barranjoey Lighthouse

A Big day for the Catamarans

Low tide in beautiful PITTWATER
Broken Bay

Jetty, Pittwater

Lion Island, BROKEN BAY

BARRANJOEY from WEST HEAD

BRISBANE WATER

Brisbane Water is the sheltered and shallow north arm of Broken Bay. It is entered by a narrow channel at its southern end and is almost landlocked. Brisbane Water's beauty is enhanced by the wooded hills that surround it. The Rip Bridge, finished in 1974, spans the narrowest part of Brisbane Water between Orange Grove near Woy Woy and Daley's Point on the east side of Brisbane Water. It provides a link between the Woy Woy district and the northern part of Brisbane Water.

The area developed slowly mainly because of poor access, but now with the Rip Bridge and the Sydney–Gosford railway it is going ahead rapidly. One development of note is St Hubert's Island, which is joined to the mainland by a concrete bridge. This project involves more than 500 homesites and some 85 per cent of these have water frontages to either the bay or to canals.

On the eastern arm of Brisbane Water is Kilcare, a popular secluded holiday resort, and the Bouddi State Park. The 1067.3 hectare park ranges along the east coast from Kilcare Beach to McMasters Beach and provides magnificent coastal scenery, wet forests and heathlands. There is also a separate section of the park at Box Head at the entrance to Brisbane Water. The Brisbane Water National Park between Brisbane Water and the Sydney–Newcastle Expressway is set in rugged sandstone country and its steep sided gorges still display remnants of a subtropical rainforest with tree-ferns and rock and tree orchids. Both of these parks have a profusion of bird life including lyre birds, parrots, cockatoos, Bell Miners and Bower birds. On the eastern seaboard north of Bouddi State Park is Avoca, a well-known holiday resort with a beautiful lake. Further north is Terrigal with its calm boathaven protected by Broken Head and the famous landmark, The Skillion, which is a long ramp of land ending in a cliff face with a rock ledge below. From here superb views of both the hinterland and the hills protecting Terrigal, and the coast, can be enjoyed. Terrigal is a well-established holiday centre and has been a major surfing venue on the central coast for more than eighty years.

Brisbane Water is one of the most beautiful recreational areas in Australia. Its beaches, lagoons and lakes, headlands, parks, forests, flora and fauna are a delight to the naturalist and to the seeker of beauty.

Empire Bay
BRISBANE WATER

Cedric Emanuel

the Rip Bridge
from Booker Bay

45

WOY WOY

Woy Woy is a small town and tourist resort on the western shore of Brisbane Water. Originally called Sandy Point, its present name is an Aboriginal word for 'deep water' or 'much water'. Four tree-covered hills— Mount Pleasant, Spion Kop, The Lookout and Blackwell Mount—provide magnificent views of the waterways below and add to the charm of Woy Woy's location.

The Sydney railway line reached Woy Woy in 1889. Just north of the town is Australia's longest railway tunnel which runs for nearly 2000 metres.

Together with its tourist industry, Woy Woy also has a commercial fishing fleet and some light manufacturing industry.

TERRIGAL
Mid North Coast N.S.W.
Cedric Emanuel

Avoca

Catamarans
Ready to race
TERRIGAL

The 685 ft. SKILLION
TERRIGAL

GOSFORD

Gosford is 89 kilometres north of Sydney at the northeast end of Brisbane Water. Surveyed in 1839 it was named after the second Earl of Gosford by the then Governor, Sir George Gipps. Samuel Peck, a rich Sydney tea merchant, built a private town of Gosford which was merged with Gosford proper in 1886. Development was slow until the Peats Ferry road was built. This cut by half the time taken to travel from Sydney. Gosford developed further when the railway came through in 1889 after the completion of the first Hawkesbury River Bridge. Gosford is now the terminus for the electric railway line from Sydney.

Tourism is a major industry in Gosford, because of the many points of interest in the area and its access to good beaches and unspoilt bushland. The world-famous Reptile Park and research station at Gosford supplies serum to the Commonwealth Serum Laboratories and similar institutions; it is also host to thousands of visitors who come each year to watch the snakes being milked. Another interesting exhibition is the recreation of Sydney as it was in 1810. Situated at Somersby, nine kilometres west of Gosford, and known as Old Sydney Town, it is rapidly becoming one of the State's best known tourist attractions.

A house of historic interest is Kendall's Cottage at West Gosford. Built in about 1838 by the Fagan Family it had become the Red Cow Inn by 1840. Henry Kendall, the poet, lived in the house for two years from 1874, and it was there that he wrote some of his best-loved lyrical verse. The building is now a museum and it has been carefully restored and maintained by the Brisbane Water Historical Society. The old Anglican church at Kincumber is also worthy of a visit from the history lover.

As well as its many tourist attractions, Gosford also produces fruit, vegetables, milk and cheese, timber and poultry. It has well-established manufacturing industries and the sandstone that is quarried there is used extensively in restoration work on many buildings of historical importance in Sydney and other centres.

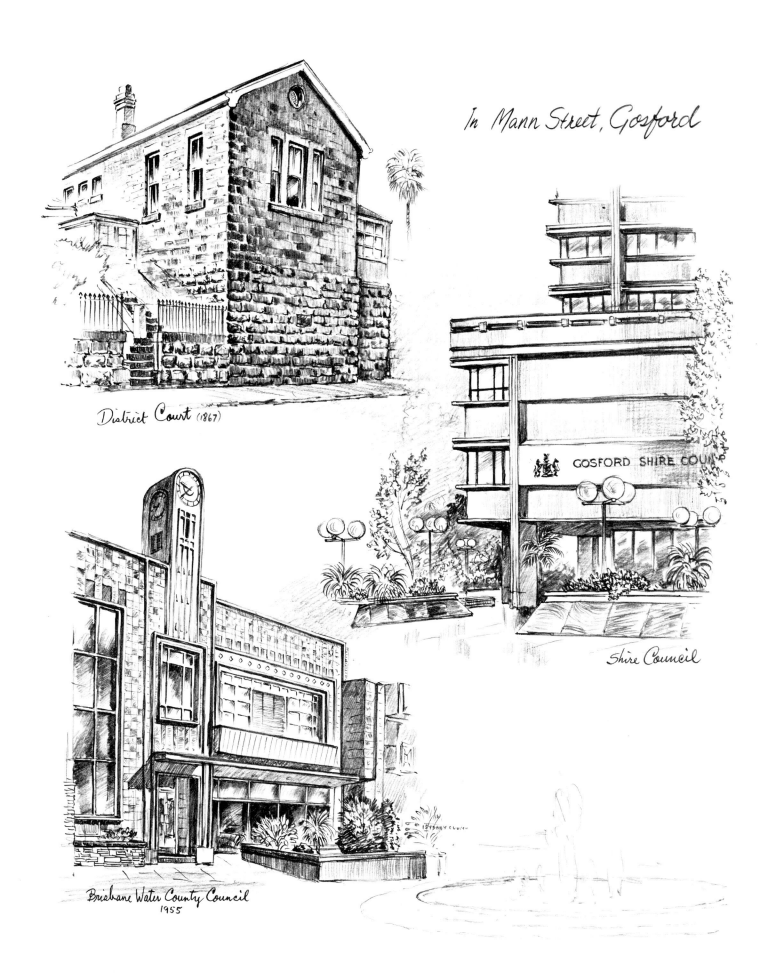

In Mann Street, Gosford

District Court (1867)

Shire Council

Brisbane Water County Council
1955

49

Anglican Church
ST PAULS 1854 KINCUMBER
Classified by the National Trust

To KENDALL'S ROCK

Henry Kendall Cottage 1838
formerly Red Cow Inn & Fagans Farm

The "PERSERVERANCE" at Boat Building Yards

Old Sydney Town

51

NEWCASTLE

Newcastle is 172 kilometres from Sydney on the Princes Highway and stands on the south side of the Port of Newcastle. The harbour—actually the mouth of the Hunter River—has been consolidated with the building of two breakwaters which extend the south and north headlands. By 1813 work had begun to join the southern shore, known as Nobby Head, to an offshore island. Convicts worked for thirty years on this breakwater. The Nobbies, as it is now known, has since been further extended.

Newcastle had its beginnings when coal was discovered there in 1791 by escaping convicts. Later, in 1797, when Lieutenant John Shortland was in pursuit of a second band of escaping convicts, he also found coal and named the Hunter River. Two years later coal was exported from the district to Bengal. A settlement of soldiers and convicts was established at Coal Harbour in 1801 by Governor King, but it was abandoned a year later. In 1804 another settlement was established and called Newcastle. It was organized as a secondary punishment gaol and the convicts were put to work as cedar-cutters, miners, and lime-burners. Convicts were not sent to Newcastle after 1824 although some stayed to work the mines.

Newcastle mined coal and progressed, but in 1913 when Broken Hill Pty Ltd began construction on a steelworks, Newcastle was on its way to becoming the second biggest industrial city in New South Wales. The first steel was produced in 1915 and now iron-smelting, steel-making and associated industries employ some 70 per cent of the town's work-force. The industrial areas are mostly located on the north side of the harbour. Both the city and the industrial section are refreshed by sea breezes and the nearby beaches lighten the city's busy industrial emphasis.

Newcastle has retained many fine public buildings of historic value. One such building is the Customs House designed by James Barnet. Completed in 1877, and built of sandstone and white Dutch bricks, it features an impressive clock tower. The Newcastle court-house, designed by Walter Vernon, was built in 1890 and the Victorian-styled Department of Public Works was built in Hunter Street in 1872. The attractive Georgian-style police station in Hunter Street was erected in 1849. Among the contemporary buildings of interest are those on the campus at the University and in the cultural centre of the city.

Customs House Clock Tower

Hunter Street, NEWCASTLE

Newcastle City Hall

53

No's 1 and 3 Laman Street
built about 1904 by Andrew Cook.

Demolished for the New
Art Gallery which was
opened 11th March 1977 by
Her Majesty the Queen

New Council Administrative Block
opened June 1977

Curie Fountain and Cultural Centre

Simpson Cottage

A National Trust Property

Old House Newcastle
Cedric Emanuel

A Reminder of the Past

Newcastle Harbour
1972 – The last of the Ferries to Stockton
KOONDOOLOO and KOOROONGABA

Civic Fountain and Cultural Centre

Simpson Cottage

A National Trust Property

Old House Newcastle
Cedric Emanuel

A Reminder of the Past

Newcastle Harbour
1972 - The last of the Ferries to Stockton
KOONDOOLOO and KOOROONGABA

'Nobbys' Newcastle
an island joined to the mainland 1854

Newcastle Beach from the scenic drive

TEA GARDENS AND HAWKS NEST

Tea Gardens is 10 kilometres off the Pacific Highway on the western shore of the Myall River mouth which drains into Port Stephens. Downstream from Tea Gardens there is a new bridge which gives access to the beautiful scenery and beaches of the small resort of Hawks Nest on the north bank of the river.

Tea Gardens is the last supply base for boatmen who plan to sail up the Myall River and enjoy the unspoilt natural wonders of the beautiful, tranquil and secluded Myall Lakes.

Timber and fishing have always been the basic industry in these two small settlements, but now tourism is also growing.

Two other waterways drain into Port Stephens—the Tilligherry Creek to the south and the Karuah River to the north west.

Little Jetty.

the sand dunes HAWKS NEST

Tea Gardens N.S.W.

Karuah River
Port Stephens

59

FORSTER AND TUNCURRY

Forster and Tuncurry are twin towns on the opposite sides of Cape Hawke Harbour, which is the entrance to Wallis Lake. The towns are linked by a long low prestressed concrete bridge built in 1959. The town of Forster was named after William Forster, who was Premier of New South Wales in 1859. Both towns offer a great deal to the tourist—fine harbour and seaside beaches, excellent fishing and boating and delightful scenery. Oyster farming and timber-getting are local industries and there is a commercial fishing fleet at Tuncurry.

The Catch

Tuncurry

61

River Boatsheds FORSTER

FORSTER — Cedric Emanuel

Tuncurry to Forster.

TAREE

Taree is delightfully situated on the Manning River, about 340 kilometres north of Sydney on the Pacific Highway. The third largest town on the North coast, it has both agricultural and manufacturing industries. Dairying and dairy products are particularly important to Taree and the four islands in the river estuary—Dumaresq, Jones, Mitchell and Oxley—are given over to this industry.

In 1831 William Wynter became the first settler in the area and in the early 1850s his son-in-law, Henry Fleet, laid out a private town on the land grant Wynter had received. This town, Taree, prospered more than the nearby official government town of Wingham. Wynter also built a ship of approximately 60 tonnes which was used extensively on river trade. However, the first ship of any real size to enter the river was the 119 tonne *Sovereign* in 1842.

Flat bottomed, slow-moving boats called droghers were used extensively in the early days of Taree. They went up and down the Manning River carrying supplies in and produce out and now are used to carry gravel from the upper reaches of the river bed.

Taree has some old and impressive civic buildings, including the Protestant Hall built in 1876 and the court house built in 1897.

Boat building, Taree
Cedric Emanuel

The last of the Dragers —
Ray Hammond's BELLBIRD — Hastings River N.S.W.
Boilers fired with wood —

PORT MACQUARIE

Port Macquarie is one of the most popular holiday resorts on the northern coast of New South Wales. It is situated at the mouth of the Hastings River and offers the tourist a wide range of water activities including good surfing. There are also many historical buildings that have been well preserved.

John Oxley discovered and named the town in 1818 in honour of Governor Lachlan Macquarie, who later described the townsite as 'a very judicious one, as combining beauty and convenience'. One of the oldest towns in New South Wales, it was a secondary place of imprisonment for convicts between 1821–1830. Soon after this free men and women settled there and, along with timber-getting, they established farms. Timber-getting has always been important to the area and still is. Sugar cane was one early crop that was to disappear and be replaced by more temperate region crops. In 1842, after a road was built from the New England district to Port Macquarie, bullock drays hauled wool and other products to Port Macquarie for shipment.

Among the buildings of historic interest is the Parish Church of St Thomas with its unusual cedar box pews. Although the church was designed by Lieutenant T. H. Owen it shows the strong influence of the colonial architect Francis Greenway. The Tacking Point lighthouse was built in 1879 on the point named by Matthew Flinders in 1802. The old lockup, thought to have been built around 1898 but now deserted, is a favourite visiting spot for tourists.

'The Monument'
from Flynn's Beach

PORT MACQUARIE

...tion PORT MACQUARIE

Lighthouse Port Macquarie

MACLEAY RIVER

The Macleay River is medium-sized and rises in the rugged forested country of the New England Plateau. The river's lower reaches pass through farming country used for vegetable and maize growing and dairying. There are also several butter and cheese factories along the river. Kempsey, about 20 nautical miles upstream, is the largest town on the river, and in 1900 a timber bridge was opened across the river there. On the south side of the Macleay River there are the small towns of Jerseyville, which has a small fishing fleet, Kinchela, Gladstone and Smithtown.

The river reaches the sea at Trial Bay which is 390 kilometres north of Sydney. The bay was named after the brig *Trial* that was owned by the Sydney merchant, Simeon Lord. It was wrecked in the bay in 1816 after it had been stolen by convicts, all of whom perished along with the crew.

A gaol was built on the headland at the bay entrance in the late 1880s to house convicts who worked on the breakwater at Laggers Point. The breakwater project became too costly, however, and in 1803 it was abandoned. The jail was used briefly for housing internees during World War I, but has not been used since.

Amateur Fishermen

Macleay River.

the remains
Trial Bay Jail (1876-86)
SOUTH WEST ROCKS
Disused since 1922

NAMBUCCA HEADS

Nambucca Heads is a pretty town situated on a hill at the mouth of the Nambucca River. Now a very popular tourist resort, it was first settled in 1842 by cedar-cutters who took the precious wood from the area for nearly thirty years. Timber-getting is still an industry there, along with fruit and vegetable growing and fishing.

The area was discovered in 1818 and in 1820 John Oxley surveyed the river entrance. The village was proclaimed in 1885 and takes its name from an Aboriginal word meaning 'entrance to the waters'.

Superb panoramic views of the coast can be seen from the lookout at nearby Yarrahapini. Yarrahapini is an Aboriginal word meaning 'native bear rolling down hill'.

The *Royal Tar* which was built on the river was initially used as a Pacific trading vessel. It was later used to take the New Australia settlers, including Mary Gilmore (later Dame) to Paraguay in the early 1900s. The New Australia settlers planned a Utopian settlement which unfortunately failed.

Nambucca Beaches

NAMBUCCA
Outlet to the sea.

Bellingen -

Nambucca River

the Pub with NO BEER.

BELLINGER VALLEY

The grassy plains of this fertile river valley are very lush. The Bellinger River joins the Kalang River on the south side of the Kalang at Urunga and these rivers share the same opening to the sea.

The Bellinger River was discovered in 1841 and the small town of Bellingen was then called Bellinger also. Bellingen is 565 kilometres north of Sydney and is situated in a fertile district where dairying, farming and timber-getting are the main industries.

Bellinger River

In the Bellinger Valley

YAMBA

Yamba is a picturesque tourist village situated on Wooli Head at the southern entrance of the Clarence River. Iluka is another small settlement on the north side of the entrance. The towns are 60 kilometres from the major centre of Grafton and they attract many people from inland farming areas to enjoy the scenery, safe surfing, fishing and boating.

The entrance to the Clarence River is currently being considered as a major deep water port for the shipment of Australian wheat overseas.

Boatsheds on the river
at YAMBA

'Morning Flight'

BRUNSWICK HEADS

Brunswick Heads is a small pretty coastal town on the south bank of the Brunswick River, about 847 kilometres from Sydney on the Pacific Highway. Brunswick Heads is circled by high rugged mountains, the river, and the sea. It is these surroundings, together with the excellent surfing and fishing, that make Brunswick Heads a very popular tourist resort.

Two breakwaters extending from the headlands and a dredged boat harbour give protection to the prawning and fishing fleets. Although Captain Henry John Rous R.M. investigated the heads in 1828 it was not settled until the 1850s.

Brunswick Heads
N.S.W.

Brunswick Heads

On the Slipo

Exit to the Sea
in big Seas.
BRUNSWICK HEADS

TWEED HEADS

Tweed Heads, originally known as Cooloon, is 894 kilometres north of Sydney on the Pacific Highway at the mouth of the Tweed River. When settled in the 1850s it was a cedar port and it is now a prosperous town because of its tourist attractions and fishing.

The hilly country behind the town offers great bushwalks and magnificent scenery. The New South Wales–Queensland border separates Tweed Heads from Coolangatta, its twin town in Queensland. The border goes out to Point Danger where there is a modern lighthouse with a laser light; a memorial to Lieutenant James Cook R.N., Captain of the *Endeavour*. Breakwaters extending from the south side of Danger Point and from the southern headland Fingal Head, give shelter to the harbour entrance. Upstream in Boyds Bay the prawn and fishing boats find a calm and secure haven.

the Tweed

Homestead in Tweed Valley

Cedric Emanuel

Fishing Boats - TWEED HEADS

NORFOLK ISLAND

Norfolk Island is a small, beautiful island situated 1063 kilometres east-nor-east from Sydney. The island's striking beauty is dramatically realized in the rugged precipitous cliffs of its coastline, its mountains with their stands of towering Norfolk pines, its fertile plains, its flora of pines, lianas, ferns and epiphytic orchids and its varied birdlife. It also has a small unpolluted beach protected by a coral reef, a mild sub-tropical climate and none of the noise or pollution of a modern city. Not surprisingly the island attracts as many as 15 000 visitors annually. Historic buildings are much in evidence; many are relics of the brutal penal settlement days when punishments were often so severe they only just stopped short of death.

The island has a fascinating history. It was discovered by James Cook in 1774 and in 1778 Captain Arthur Phillip sent Lieutenant Philip Gidley King with a party of twenty-two convicts and marines in the *Supply* to establish a settlement there. More convicts and soldiers

followed and by 1790 there was a severe shortage of food. The cost of conducting a penal settlement there became so onerous that it had been abandoned by 1813. It was revived in 1825 and the gaol and many large stone buildings were built as was its reputation for being the worst place of inhumane punishment. It again ceased to be a penal settlement in 1854, and two years later 194 Pitcairn islanders arrived from their own crowded island to settle there. Later forty-six of these islanders returned to Pitcairn because they were homesick. Today the descendants of the Pitcairners on Norfolk Island account for about one third of the population there.

Norfolk Island was a separate British colony of Britain but in 1896 it became a dependency of New South Wales and in 1913, a territory of Australia. In 1973 restoration of the historic buildings began and is still continuing. For dramatic and beautiful scenery this naturalist's Eden of Norfolk Island is unsurpassed.

The Convict Settlement
NORFOLK ISLAND

Quality Row
NORFOLK ISLAND

HISTORIC Bloody Bridge
NORFOLK ISLAND

Cedric Emanuel

A house on Norfolk Island — now occupied by a descendant of Fletcher Christian

The old Salt House
NORFOLK ISLAND.

Cedric Emanuel
1976

ST BARNABAS CHAPEL
The Church of England
NORFOLK ISLAND

Recovered 1973
'SIRIUS' Anchor

On 19th March 1790 the 'SIRIUS' flagship of the
First Fleet was wrecked on the reef at Kingston
during the first settlement.

NORFOLK ISLAND

Cedric Emanuel

Civil Hospital

the Commissariat Stores 1835
Major Anderson 50ᵗʰ Reg. Commandant

Prisoners Barracks
'Gallows Gate'

Convict Store 1826

Old Mill

Watch Tower

Bakehouse

Reminders of the Penal Days NORFOLK IS.

CAPTAIN WRIGHT
OF THE 39th REGIMENT

To commemorate the death of Private John Shearman of his detachment who became the untimely victim of a disease produced by a trifling accident

1798 HADDINGTON
Killed by a whale

Hny Knowls
who was EXECUTE on the 22nd of SepT 1834 Aged 29 yrs

Thos Saulsbury WRIGHT
of Yorkshire 1843 aged 105 years and got the 'cat' when 95

James Faye
Christian stop and meditate on this man's sad and awful fate on earth No more he breathes again... He lived in hope... But died in pain

William Tandy
SOLDIER
after many years faithful service was drowned in Emily Bay 1845

A Container of contemporary articles was sealed in this wall on 11th Oct 1974 Bi Centenary Celebrations To be opened 10th Oct 2074

Lieutenant PHILIP GIDLEY KING
ROYAL NAVY
together with 7 free persons 6 female convicts and 9 male convicts landed near this spot on 6th March 1788 to form the 2nd. British settlement in the South Pacific

Walter Burke
Native of County Tipperary Who was executed for the mutiny on this island on September 22nd 1834 aged 28 Years
Lord have mercy on his soul

Thomas York
aged 22 years
Who was accidently shot by a brother soldier on the night of 17th January 1839 whilst in pursuit of mutineers engaged with others in a disgraceful attempt against the peace of the settlement on the morning of the 15th day of the same month

Frank Warren
Native of Providence U.S.A. Brutally murdered by a Greek miscreant on board ship Hope August 11, 1861 in the 18th year of his life

John Baid
Late private in Queen's Own Regiment who was accidentally drowned while on duty (as one of the guard) by the upsetting of a boat off the harbour on 1st of August 1835

History told oddly at Norfolk Island

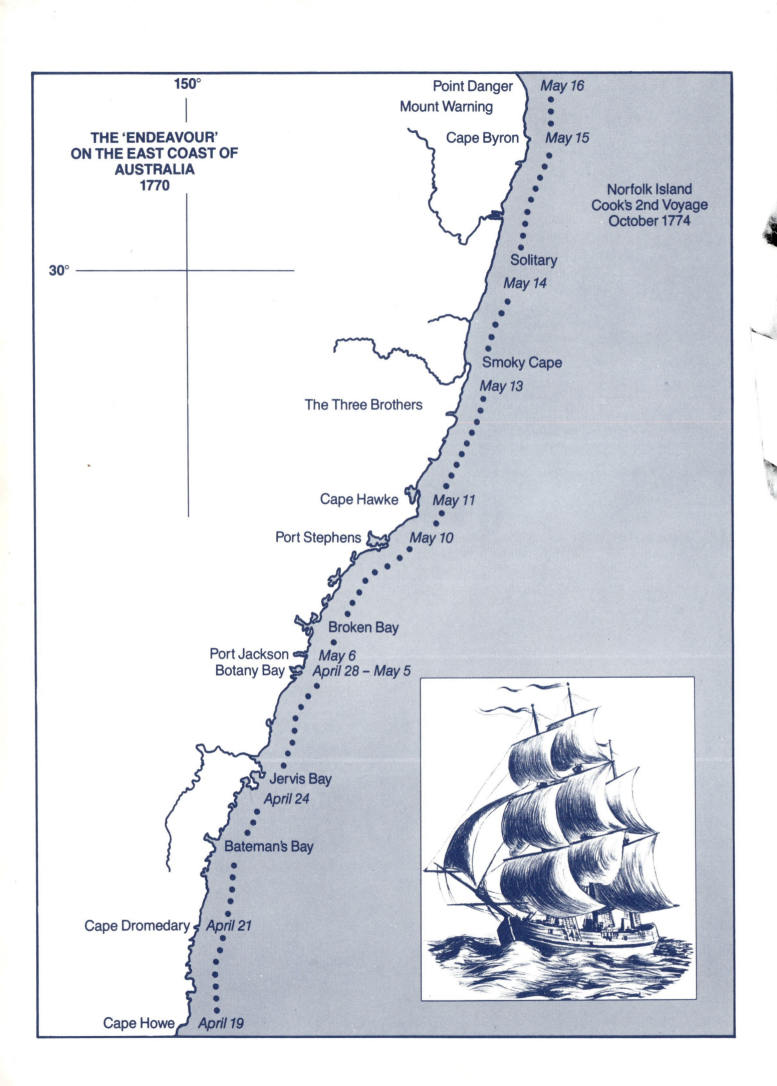

**THE 'ENDEAVOUR'
ON THE EAST COAST OF
AUSTRALIA
1770**

150°

30°

Point Danger
May 16
Mount Warning
Cape Byron
May 15

Norfolk Island
Cook's 2nd Voyage
October 1774

Solitary
May 14

Smoky Cape
May 13

The Three Brothers

Cape Hawke
May 11

Port Stephens
May 10

Broken Bay

Port Jackson
May 6
Botany Bay
April 28 – May 5

Jervis Bay
April 24

Bateman's Bay

Cape Dromedary
April 21

Cape Howe
April 19